D1190300

WATERWORN

WATERWORN

for Ted with admiration

Star Black

from star

A GATHERING OF THE TRIBES
FLY BY NIGHT PRESS
NEW YORK

ACKNOWLEDGMENTS

Grateful acknowledgement is made to the editors of the following
publications where portions of *Waterworn* first appeared: Martin Tucker
of *Confrontation*, "[Sepia];" Michael Carter of *Redtape*, "[Transfers],"
"[Marooned]," "[Yawn]," "[Insurrections]," "[Ghosts]," "[Drenched];" Evelyn
Horowitz, Michael Malinowitz and Mary Du Passage of *Bad Henry Review*,
"[Harlequins]," "[Dauntless]," "[Misfired]," "[Breath]," "[Old Days]," "[Lost],"
"[Howdy]," "[Inseparate];" Brendan Lorber of *Lungfull*, "[Decisions,
Decisions]," "[Hazed];" Steve Cannon of *Gathering of the Tribes*, "[Numb];"
and John Farris of *Sensitive Skin*, "[Chastened];" and the Bond Street
Theater Company and Palenville Interarts for providing the place where
this poem was written. *Waterworrn's* opening and closing couplets are
from Shakespeare's Sonnets LXXIV and CLIV, respectively.

Library of Congress Catalogue Card Number 95-61256

A GATHERING OF THE TRIBES SERIES #7
Edited by Hal Sirowitz
in association
with
FLY BY NIGHT PRESS,
P.O. BOX 20693, THOMPKINS SQUARE STATION,
NEW YORK, NEW YORK 10009

Cover photo by Jonathan Quinn, Mid-Atlantic #2 © 1992
Author photo by Peggy Eliot © 1993
Book design by Mary Carlson

ISBN 09639585-3-4

WATERWORN

WATERWORN

I

[Cascade]	1
[Harlequins]	2
[Numb]	3
[Tinker Street]	4
[Gorgon]	5
[Suttee]	6
[Thin Light]	7
[Shadow Plays]	8
[Paradise]	9
[Woodstock]	10
[Misfired]	11
[Decisions, Decisions]	12
[Blown]	13
[Bound]	14
[Hazed]	15
[Sepia]	16
[Trance]	17
[Short Circuit]	18
[Locale]	19
[Breath]	20
[Screened]	21
[Old Days]	22
[Free Lance]	23

II

[En Passant]	27
[Grasmere]	28
[Dauntless]	29
[Oh Well]	30
[Ripped]	31
[No Way]	32
[Howdy]	33
[Di]	34
[Inseparate]	35
[Chastened]	36
[Domesticity]	37
[Shush]	38
[Unsigned Valentine]	39
[Acid Rain]	40
[Slashed Prices]	41
[Floundering]	42
[Intercession]	43
[Lost]	44
[Exposed]	45

[Moiré] 46
[Mute] 47

III
[Blue Island] 51
[Éspanôl] 52
[Coronado] 53
[Gutted] 54
[Dark Age] 55
[Pin Dots] 56
[Nova Spies] 57
[Shop Talk] 58
[Spare Time] 59
[Migrant] 60
[Transfers] 61
[Marooned] 62
[Mauka] 63
[Downcast] 64
[Retreat] 65
[Flight Plans] 66
[Womb Water] 67
[Yawn] 68
[Taboo] 69
[Roe Wade] 70
[Soundless] 71

IV
[Drenched] 75
[Undone] 76
[Mimicries] 77
[Lulled] 78
[Insurrections] 79
[Clasped] 80
[Cadenza] 81
[Tidy] 82
[Sidekicked] 83
[Stranded] 84
[Sanctum] 85
[Ghosts] 86
[Makai] 87
[Roundrobin] 88
[Posted] 89
[Ethereal] 90
[Sweet Dreams] 91

"The worth of that is that which it contains,
And that is this, and this with thee remains."

[Cascade]

Bashed back to plain speak from yellowing
water lilies scooped out of frog-rippled ponds
where the underwear of bathers not yet in love
clings in translucent nylon to the skin wet
from spring-chilled waterfall spray, to be
poured through a wall to not anyone but you
in order to converse, makes verse memoranda

and, rather than count the zeroes of the universe
to find an emptiness mirroring the perfection
of this genderless communion, I regress, throw
off my shoes and formless flowerchild dress,
keeping covered only enough not to alarm you,
and with a sadness that comes from turning away
worlds to think a little longer, slip into water.

[Harlequins]

Now that so many wands have waved
scarfs into canes, juggled eggs, worn
the treads of unicycles to smooth rubber,
now that the eyebrowed glasses with
the pug nose are off, we hardly know
each other, frumps in our floppy shoes,
even though you always say we know
much more than we've needed to and

it's too late, all's clown paint, magic.
These caravans that nudge the hands
through small towns, revolving oranges,
stilts in the van, remove nakedness to
rooms that take for granted truth, and,
without props or colors, demythologize.

[Numb]

The tender-hearted, stepping over derelicts
to reach the library, balance the smallest
budgets neatly, fearing random audits, high
rents, defaults. And, as the bus driver leaps
to his feet to call "What was that? I didn't
hear you" to a grudge who complained about
exact change too long, break-dancers fade

on the library steps until their fast-talk
tunes are inaudible, and unaccomplished
errands become an entire afternoon. Blocks
from soup kitchens and flea-bagged rooms,
brick walls laundering the slumped with
sun, there's more than enough tidying up
to do, more creviced dust for any broom.

[Tinker Street]

Days slip from the calendar and spill
into urgencies. Hasty remarks leave the
dumbfounded awake, while the stoned stare
into space from prim park benches: war
resisters, heavy thinkers, cut-off hems
shred and tattered, beards in place.

Their wire rims circulate within
coiling air, the deep transparencies there,
mandalas of the universe expanding between
the ears, years of mandalas, expanded fears.
You pick up your pen name, hurl it through
wildflower bushes and purple haze onto

the tiny New Age square. Teenagers scrap
it, toss it away, like a flyer to nowhere.

[Gorgon]

Medusa, tangle me in snakes. Turn lakes
to stone, fish to jade, marble my moods,
decapitate my pain, enslaved by swords
whipped by the brawn of heroes, and cast
a yowl onto fear, breath cloud of mirrors,
so my face recedes into interiors of now
freed from misconceptions of your image,
cast through time like iodine swallowed

by my sex, as if to apologize for defeat;
then, let me be, as the turned cheek of the
Nazarene, meek, untroubled, loving, for we
have seen too much chivalry, the violent
sham of victory: beheaded, hoisted above
drenched battlefields of frightened eyes.

[Suttee]

Too formal to fail you, the circling moon
an absentee calling me by my mother's
name, thistled by earlier survival, I step
forward through the cautioning century
on hastily laid planks of wood to breathe
the fire cloud like opium, a ceremony
planned by happenstance in childhood.

You rise, a Finnegan grumbling to the crowd,
and lead me back to the netted village where
thimbly lamps sway in the heat, then brush
the soot from my singed garments, as if to
release me from further incarnations, and,
in a trance of salutations preserved by the
deceased, undo tradition with your hands.

[Thin Light]

The lazy gunfire of dawn saps my energy
and the mind in kind surrenders the tease,
iotas of flesh unforgotten by the police,
always too blue for minor tragedies. Fleas
fuss in the blacking skeletons of trees
and toss their humming ironies into the
cabins as the raccoons quiet down, garbage
hunters masked for the revelry of hunger.

You wonder why all presidents but Nixon
have blue eyes but dismiss the premonition
as if caught in the billowing lies of madness.
Too many public health officials are ensnarled
in the gridlock of psychosis, prefabbing new
locations for misfits under the brittle skies.

[Shadow Plays]

I'm always gooey when I fantasize, castled
in glass, tremulously wrong about reality,
as far from the minute hand as myth to money,
and I don't understand manly certitudes or
wish to confuse you with my issues exactly
because you have your own fantasizing to do
and I can't intrude, but for me to admit that
you're completely absent would be inaccurate.

There are limits to separateness, blurry limits,
limits no man knows I suppose if you want to
be separate about it, lulling drifts and shifts
of limits, to wax eloquent from afar. I could
verbalize less, doze in careful silences, but
at least fantasies give inklings to who we are.

[Paradise]

To return to underdeveloped islands and see
all the new electricity, radios and televisions
that once were oil lamps, splash baths and
gamelans, dim-lit hamlets mystical and bare,
is to lift the rose-rimmed vision and stare at
details airbrushed from brochures on our time,
not theirs. Tours, illusionary sojourns to hidden
Edens with jumbo tarmacs and group fares,

trailmark corrupted intrusions of progress
into thoroughfares of disappointment until
all tourists complain the island is no longer
the same as it was before they arrived, and
because of all the tacky new disconcerting
modern amenities, they will not come back.

[Woodstock]

He looks like Racquel Welch's last husband,
grooved features haggard, forlorn. He plays
horn with stubbled blues rockers time capsuled
from the massive festival that haunts curio shops
and beleaguered barns, smokes between takes.
I see the heyday of my generation break the
haze as middle-aged ghosts, stained gauze
bandaging mental casualties, I, for one.

People say why doesn't your generation
flatten the unenlightened nerds who ruin
this nation, k.o. 'em like a crazed heavyweight?
and I always say because we haven't recovered
just yet, as if, with full Jeffersonian power,
we'd turn the world around, make it work.

[Misfired]

I lost you, your spare parts shelved in an airport
locker I never got to open with the smallest key,
the plane must've crashed, disintegrated me, or
it never took off because there wasn't a cab or bus
in that someday day to transport our geographies
to a dot, even though you'd bought used welcome
mats with threshold thoughts, as the sun rusted
lowercased rooftops of the napping town at dusk.

These constant returns to what never was burn
off the damp mists of early morning, shadows
of tree trunks draw back into themselves as if
to hide, our betrayals were too inept to survive
the struggles of reconstruction, even though the
town's skyline was so low, humble, uncluttered.

[Decisions, Decisions]

Are you torn between being a woman or an artist?
Don't be, don't be an artist. There really is no such
occupation though I'm in the minority opinion, much
like the septuagenarian supreme court justice who
presents an astoundingly compassionate dissent as
the retarded go to the guillotine and vasectomies
are never mentioned, it's meaningless, my opinion,

it never wins an argument with a painter or clown.
I've no easel or skit, I'm frightened of the public,
and if you've a neurosurgical problem I can't fix it,
but this way, no matter what your chromosomes,
you're seldom drafted, often left alone, can avoid
being battered if you know how to use the phone,
and storms, ships, moons and darkness honor you.

12

[Blown]

While you, lotused in petals, fell from the sky
as a Buddha of precautions, onto the tiny gold-
leafed altar that keeps my trespasses from
wandering far, I, agonged by the sunflowered
silence of it all, mutely impressed, fell into
particles of hopelessness. "We have to be our
own wives," Sona said. A worried household

rattles under typhooned showers, snapping
wires, shutting things off, the consolations
of solitude lighting more candles than needed;
but oh, apropos to the starry opuses, my home
ascended then settled, and so many doors have
fallen from your petals all the walls are open,
windowing the compass with flusters of trees.

[Bound]

I'm glad you believe in this dither of the subkingdom,
the protozoan soul flicked out like a Frisbeed disc
onto the stencilled ad infinitums of the universe
to nick a curious sun, because for you I sing, badly.

And if this lisp of gramarye is decoded by aliens,
who can forecast their archeologies? their wing-
tipped need to learn from lonely solariums? We
fax our testimonials, spiderwebbed by telephones,

and, like dinosaurs in tar, descend, yet if we don't
know who we are what can we expect of them?
They have left us alone with a globe, more than
enough documentation to go either way: on and on

or out. I think most protozoa want to stay and I
stay with you whose lips echo something endless.

[Hazed]

Fear, the catchword of distress, wonderlands every
movement unless some luminant expert whisks all your
hesitations away, clarifying hurt, and, in this absence
of visible scars, all the operations and car crashes

that make a body worth sleeping with (I'm timid
about all this), there you are, caught in the wrong
nightie, unrelaxed, requesting a glass of water or
brew, wondering what other women do that is so

right, so intoxicating and tender, surely they were
destined to many more surrenders than you ever knew
which is why they aren't shut up in a dark room

explaining it all, but I'm getting confused. Fear
doesn't contain enough facts, it tends to be hazy,
inexact, a fog you're constantly sifting through.

[Sepia]

Heterosexual love poetry's like Art Deco, an urban
professional fad for Retro, an old refinished radio
salvaged from a musty apartment that isn't stereo

enough to use, but beautiful, something to match
the black porcelain tableware that makes your dinner
parties a bit unusual: it assembles a mood, evokes

a stranded memory from adolescence, some erotic
embarrassment that made you shy before you were
widowed by proms and indelible caution, a fumbled

unfastening that awoke in awkward strokes desire.
Now, behind toppled dominoes of disappointment, we
misprint what's lost yet everlasting, as if we still

wore slips to slip off or there was still that barn,
that dark entangled crush of straw, that hayloft.

[Trance]

Closed chapters of innocence, and it's just as well
in the long enervating summer light skittering toward
chilly burials of snow, to growl a bit, boast in the lull,

embellish ghost stories in the secret hideout with
some snazzy adjectives. No apologies are needed, what
scares can soothe, for in that crackling bear-clawed

night encircling the shivering flashlight when sounds
wrangle from the underground to gobble secrets for food
and you are in charge of the spooky narrative that

narrates you, staccatos of the sublime percolate
windy vowels engulfing the bobbling battery'd glow,
languaging the spirits, and, as shaman on call,

you live up to it, if only to mediate between the visible
and invisible instant that, when melded, enthralls.

[Short Circuit]

A flute, played with a mediocrity that could only be live,
is driving me wild in this now humanized wilderness,
rendering Zen uneternal for the moment like a traffic

jam, yet, pausing meekly, can I disturb it, assert myself
as an experiential graduate with boundaries who can now set
limits, convey a communication without being destructive

either to myself or to the maker of music? Can I do what
no child has ever known? No, that's why we've never met.
I'm too timorous, and your mind is so set on occupations

of regret that a meeting wouldn't fit the vaporous schedules
that convey our weeks like a ship with black sails, I guess,
in melodramas of deprivation. The flute is quiet, I've lived

through the crisis like a phobic with a psychiatrist, made
progress, worked out this blameless tremor of distress.

[Locale]

Heaving the 'I' in a trash bin for a sociological spin
through nouvelle callousness that is making all
our restaurants international south of south Bronx –
a delicious Vietnamese egg roll of amnesia, meaty

Tibetan noodles spiced by the dispossessed – our
only hope is that activists, too tired from the day's
frustrations to read much, might skim thin volumes
to renew their resistance to the glaringly obvious,

while the fashion industry, valiumed on style
to keep pace with revolving seasons of advertising
space, sleeps in roomy cooperatives that have made
simple dwellings passé. Shall we move south,

chuck this biz for a clapboard house by a creek,
winnow and fish? Nobody busy is stopping us.

[Breath]

If I could snatch back all the harsh words bashed
out of my bagged lady past and hurled via a friendly
postal clerk to the quiet side of our country, I would
stop that acid rain chemically combined by mental

instability from falling, but I was recklessly unstrung
in a Versailles of the mind and the mirrors ricocheted
like atoms, heated to the brink, and multiplied. I took
action but mistook the time. I was too impatient to

reach you though I tried, in the delusional quicksand
of an obsession, to break out and, with that first crack
of light, survived the cutting floor of narcissism,

and this isn't the monkey's paw at your door, but an
appreciation, as if words were sufficient to thank anyone
who pulls you from unstoppable suffocations of fire.

[Screened]

Rather misspell than spell out, wasn't raised on honesty
but veneer, manipulations that endear getaways to teens.
Mighty uncomfortable at home those locked-in years when
you learn to smoke to get out of the house, constellations

behind the garage flustering about in the dark like pals
before fresh starts were known to mankind, an antediluvian
state of mind where troubles are too amorphous to define
and nobody wants you to, grades are what's in view, track

medals. But everyone I know no longer smokes or ponders
like a nostalgic over these obstacles, a sandbox treadwater
of sorts, very backyard, unsolvable, so I hesitate to invite

you through this army-brat door screen into the kitchen
of my youth for a Velveeta snack since, given the shambled
emotions held back, it wouldn't take you long to leave.

[Old Days]

If you're married when you read this you won't read it
so I have nothing to worry about, the blither's homefree,
I would hope you worlds away, sheltered in illiteracy, and
unlike Sting I wouldn't expect you to remember me. I'm

one of those Wildean women men forego for matrimony,
thanking their lucky stars they were wise enough to think
twice, destined for occasional recollection on an occasional
night when, after being so happy for so long, sate of love,

births and security, a mild hurricane of feeling wisps in,
reminding them of a sad vacation they took once on the dunes
to get over some intangible tragedy. It passes, as a crescent

moon of wine in a glass vanishes, leaving a pleasant aura
of safety. This was the sacrificial self I withered in
on those same sad dunes before I knew how to resist.

[Free Lance]

Wandering through the anatomy of the lagoon, a womb
of unfamiliar serenity, it dawned on me no one I know well
is dying lately except Stephen and Craig and Paul, particularly
Stephen whose cancer broke out in June, but a catheter's

been put in, so he may not be back to the hospital soon,
leaving no overwhelming anxiety to ruin the moment. And here,
peeled from the city like repulsive wallpaper and transported
to a retreat which was once a nunnery with modest white

spiritual statues hidden in the woods, I feel almost,
but not entirely, free, unburdened by the stramash of money,
its debilitating need, and I want to thank somebody,

as if blessings limned in litanies were actual, manifest
in a holy timeless gratuity unknown to me because I'm always
too busy to look, see, feel, hear, help any other but me.

[En Passant]

Yo, you step on my stationery after busting out
of the penitentiary to accuse me of Jessica Hahning
your cell after you nameless-feared me to hell, well,
which feminist perspective to take here? Jezebel?

Cinderella? You're bootprinting my concentration. I
need time to unwind the latest Wiccan spell to terrify
you a second time, flash my dark side to flabbergasted
guards, or are you trying to pen me a Valentine? Oh

no, it's just my hubris spieling a monologue with 'you'
pasted on it like a ransom note and there is no stationery
or boot, and you've never been a criminal in your life,

just a nice cheerful inordinately kind type guy who,
while out walking one balmy day, minding your business,
was nearly vivisected by a huge, ferocious female bat.

[Grasmere]

Tired of tentacles and twat, eager to elope the city,
unsettled by this hippified resurgence of sound that
repels Eton with crudity, I sigh in dizzying rewinds
of what once was Tintern Abbey, quiet mysticisms

of lakes exempt from condominiums and slavery, 'ere
the dawn of sitcoms and films, when stream-flushed
groves were wildly shadowed and had no mosquitos.
But it was a minor diary'd world of devoted sisters,

although chimney sweeps gave soot its due in thin
songs. Now, when a message on a machine shatters
a week, and half the nearest population is plagued,
there are fewer coach-rolled retreats, more newsy

items to stash away, and to just John Wayne along as
stolid pioneers is to lose our heritage. One, anyway.

[Dauntless]

I love it when you get so fleshy, we should ditch this
gig, phone a motel but will you recognize me? Doubtful,
I could spend the night in an adjacent room while you
conclude I've stood you up and hate yourself for agreeing

to an inane rendezvous of cheap neon-lit sheets when
you could've been home working alone, controlling things,
whereas I, blinded by the latest Batman, would wait
anxiously wringing my hands thinking you'd driven off

a bridge or didn't really want to see me but didn't know
how to dump me gently so decided not to cancel until it
was too late, yet if you weren't so bruised and bashful

I wouldn't be waiting here in the first place, caught
in an endless circle. What a date. I'd still go, though,
given these and other highly likely innumerable risks.

[Oh Well]

Only your best friends tell you you're an egoist,
rejected like anyone else. Abandonment's so toney
these days, so apropos to sex. It deadened me, just
in time for dysfunctional to describe everything.

You saw the table move, levitate above the cat
then twirl around, happens a lot in Motown, but once
gravity gelled and all the bouncing molecules fell

back into place, you moved, with a sort of stumbling
grace, right along, and why do I care? because I'm alone,
wavering in loops on the crowded cobblestone, or

with the detachment of accommodation, curious
about you, at least here and elsewhere too, have been
since I saw you (this drivel's true), but if you insist
we're through, fine. I'm too tired or blind to argue.

[Ripped]

I drank and stank, reeked of inhalations, poured
everything into the emptied mansion then tottered
about in a feathered robe complaining there's no one
worthy enough to let in and, then, rather than passing

out like a dignified degenerate, called friends,
and there will be no end to that slur-slopped binge,
that loss of numbers. Now, joining the lengthening
statistic of bummers, the world offers suspicious

forgiveness and clouds of doubt but I no longer
blame it, burn down the house, or strut around in
snooty overtones of intellect, feigning disinterest,
polishing my nails (I never did that), brushing flecks

of dust from fatal interviews, combing my hair
famously into mirror after mirror after mirror.

[No Way]

Like apologies floating into an open grave, we save
good things to say for last. In what family of experience
did it become so benumbed, love, what unintended or intended
iciness drove us back to silences that now seem sad

or are these flowered rituals on the hill the only chance
we have to talk things through, a strange location, I might
add, when we could start earlier, but, still and uninterrupted,
as if the closely mowed grass were a green reservoir

of buried forgiveness, all our compliments and kisses
tumbling into it, a kind of loving that can only begin
after it is finished, communicated above marble

in passionate adieus, tenderness breaking through in torrents.
Maybe the upper hand's so important we wait to see who outlasts
who before we speak, but that's too much waiting for me.

[Howdy]

Philosophies of the fanfare bring me back to you.
It's too empty in the overpopulated vacuum not
to want a companion or at least an intersection
among the traffic of greens and blues to pastel,

waterdown bulky hills with a Chinese brush stroke,
though I feel the laughingstock of the western world
returning to you, I the flicked-off moth from the bulb
of your mind, yet, unlike businessmen I've known, you

offer more to rivalry than neglect and it was me who
was unkind. Wish I hadn't been so overwhelmed by men
when you happened along (long story), but who times

these collisions properly? I believe I'll soon leave this
portion of the sky for a sunbelt trailored by retirees,
a safety-measure spot, with some cranky tornadoes.

[Di]

My father made me never question love, he was
a pys-ops criminal on the shuffledown to our hometown
scales of Nuremberg, lots of Nam and spooky business
north of the delta, but he couldn't find any place

to pay him to go to school but the Point, besides,
in ways warped by naiveté, he was a patriot of sorts,
at least he thought he was serving his country like some
southerner once thought, charging the barricades made

ironic by Pol Pot, rancid by Tricky Dick and deathly sick
by the scalpel of Jayavarman who enslaved half his
nation to build himself a few magnificent face-lifts,

Ankor Wat, hardly appreciated by French-educated
communists but wonderful art. I don't know why my father
was so attentive and loving to his kids but he was.

[Inseparate]

And now I'm crying for him because he's dead I guess
although that curtain between us is so thin I don't notice
it much, he's just away again, working out some happy
strategy to save the world and keep men free, who

knows what he is or isn't doing so far away from me,
I just believe in returns, so when my mother said he visited
her, walked right into the living room to talk (she had a few
apologies to do) I said wonderful, I'm glad he rose from

the dead to lend a helping hand to your severed regrets
and hoped the meeting went well. She looked tired, afraid
I'd think she was crazy, but for a change I believed her

since those channels have helped me too. I've also been
visited years ago by a friend who hurried through my heart
although, before then, nothing seemed hurried at all.

[Chastened]

There's so much healing going on the air's thick
with the pus of gauze, I doodled your Bible and I
was wrong but from what zoo do we all come? My
arrows now break on the sea and the weekend has

vanished into the week, like a girl's papered princess
all my glitter's smudged away to an Elmer's glue
thumbed profile of a fairytale de Kooninged by you,
could the illusion have endured any other way?

The venom you say punctures innocents, vaccinates
the sick, but I scrawled Jarrell's lipstick over your
name and I'm to blame for an inconsiderateness

that dismisses restraint, nobody can make love
that way, so when you ducked out in your powerboat
like a prince to breathe alpine lakes, I changed.

[Domesticity]

How come cats can relax? If I didn't
bring home the bacon my cat couldn't be
an independent woman but she doesn't
realize how much is entailed in getting

her cans of Super Suppers opened since
all she does is nod and nap, give herself
a lot of baths, then snuggle up for more
naps while this hard-bitten household

honcho is mired in gridlock or therapy,
never takes naps, snuggles up to nobody,
and can't even come home to collapse
without opening more Super Supper cans

then going to the faucet for running water;
she likes hers running instead of bowled.

[Shush]

You have a weird job, and I've heard enough
of your tide pools, fizzling perfumes and dolls,
I have a life to lead in the alligator's mouth
too, without your pilgrimed moanings, though,

I agree, to be a buffoon's hard, but look at me:
a nymph in lockjaw clamped by sticky palmettos,
I'm swamped and unreconciled constantly and
I want to come home, throw up my claws.

People who stay together don't say anything
to each other anymore, conversations run out,
Magna Cartas of silence support the house,

whereas we're pitched out back, zippered
together in a sleeping bag, and do nothing but
schmooze, bicker and yak. Some meadow.

[Unsigned Valentine]

Oh. A cookie cutter heart. Smart. I have
a cookie cutter heart too, but it's shut up.
Now, this dank musk takes flour out of
baking, chocolate chips so delicious all

gone, everywhere grown ups all grown.
I have a rubberband ring with rhinestone,
jacks and a top, spun spun. Who locked
the lock, who locked, who knocked? You

can come out. "Little Sally Ann, sitting
in the sand, weeping and crying for her
man. Rise, Sally, rise, wipe your dirty

eyes, turn to the right and turn to the
left and turn to the one who you love
the best." Boo. Bet you can't catch me...

[Acid Rain]

They used to say our trade was dangerous and it is,
the endangered gravitate to flames as grizzlies did.
As aborigines bushed with sticks hurled them toward
conquistadors without mercy, we take some risks

yet days of Buddhistic mindfulness bring us escape
and we believe in days, eternities, moments. Seductions
of boredom, its sleek arrogance monochroming all vistas,
disinterests us, lets us down in some boorish manner,

yet there are conspiracies against our bridges and ovens
that have viewed the entire occupation as sick, revulsive,
and only incoming tides of religions lapse through our

losses, keeping us all on the beach in fallouts of radiation,
huddled close with cans of surplus and bottled water,
whispering in the heat together, plotting reversals.

[Slashed Prices]

So, birthday candles that crunch our souls into
shattering molds of maturity are still counted
long after their questionable tabulations sliced
our age, until to grow old is so dreary, so opposite

the savored waterfalls of Kool cigarettes and
beers, we no longer endear ourselves to layering
years happily, fearing wrinkles or weight, whatever
we're told to hate about ourselves so shopping

malls stay open on Sunday. Oh, may I lie with you
on your bed of nails and close my eyes for a while
until the holiday sales are over, until all used cars

are resold and the plastic recycled. Asia, where
garbage bags were made of paper, seems so far away,
my home's there, or on some boat-peopled isle.

[Floundering]

Vespal oddities: protestants have never been good
at ideas; protesting ideas yes, having them no. Our
roots are leaves scattered on mounds of ideologies,
but to be aware of our ineptness counts, and we've

flamed a few, not enough, liberties with a flair for
mispronunciation only the grateful forgive, a birth-
mark on this tan-endangering skin, a confirmation
before spires fell to the wind in a swoosh of steepled

intolerances that render the mind homeless, scratching
club-footed golf courses with fingernailed persistence,
the hapless bigotries that quilt with sutures of fear
this nation, though we can pray anywhere which helps.

It is impossible to defend blackened galleys of men
and token girls we brought into this continuing mess.

[Intercession]

The worst photo assignment I've had, oh forget it,
it would take too long to explain why I couldn't
follow-focus for a newspaper what would be too
repelling to record and emotionally impossible,

a jumper on the Empire State, and as I tried to
be a committed professional and slunk that way
nauseously, I found a crisis cop had talked him
down. I walked up to this scruffy young Irishman

like Mary Magdalene and gazed as the heavens
exploded and all the fire engines rumbled away,
back to their sheltered caverns of inaction, and

asked, my career reprieved from retirement, how
he did it, and he said "the guy just wanted to talk
to his father and we told him we could arrange it."

[Lost]

What I miss most that the commune of marriage holds,
besides the luxury of pennilessness, is grocery lists
and crumpled clothes that crimp fear into manageable
chores, the boring commonplace rituals that must be

performed; it's sad, if more efficient, doing them alone.
But in this mutinied tortoiseshell home, ivy'd by kelp
coloring the rips, the self can, as a genie, slip back
to invisibility, grumbling and mumbling as it goes,

until it's but a hiss whisking mullions from windows,
not enough to break down walls, but mist the glass some
for fingercloud painting, but my tenure's running out,

the semesters crowd me in these slippered hours
and I need some outfield to slouch in, ever expectant,
those loined curfews that make gardens from stone.

[Exposed]

Polaroids, palettes, oils, yours, fall to the floor,
sapping my envy. My languid rolls on the rug
leave nothing on those lushly composed squares
but I've never belonged there, undressed and

listless, the mannered odalisque in me resists
that eternalizing eye contact, that bagatelled
compliance, all the sleepwalked halls jabbered
in. Atop Kali's skulls, another trinity broadens

the indeterminable horizon, spinning the great
wheel through my fictions, evoking a vastness
that excludes nothing, no one. You may snap

velvet vacuums that dematerialize my bones,
I am nowhere, near no settee or stair, casual
jewels dripping from no long tussled hair.

[Moiré]

Leaves, velveting the night with heartlessness,
unfasten this misbegotten magnificence that
obeys no name, lift the pain it causes from cold
slate, let it rustle, disintegrate into harmless

insignificance, collapse as pickup sticks into
a jumble of lines, cylindered, hidden in a closet
which should never see light, my boudoir, my night

sketches. We work alone under your changing
addresses, shifted by air into sound, patterbound
whisperings. We need no one personally for this

effort, but inevitably seek company, a friend.
I should have pleased the leaves instead, leaves
that canopy my bed, gone on and on in the thickening
darkness, a heartlessness that makes us dead.

[Mute]

Tears tears tears, they've flown enough, we
cry for ourselves no longer. In this dainty century
of bad stuff that rendered poetry impossible, a steel
survival seals the sentimental and, in the wrecked

expanse, tidal-waved by horror, stares, skeletoned
in genocides and drugs, aware, equipped for nonviolent
war against what sickens mountains, strips us
of compassion, yet to type this is meaningless.

I hide from leaders, duck out to walk hills,
critiquing responsibilities assumed by others
like a spectator sports fan at the tube. Language

contains very few, we talk but do not do, recite
actions through, or become breathless to convey
restraint as if the only word left was stop.

[Blue Island]

Great men postpone my demise, trammel
me with truths or lies, keep me awake, disguised,
bluestockinged by synthetics. I look into their eyes
to see what's become, what's to become of me, and find

more time, as the lyric dives quietly
into the pool of narrative, ripples and dies. A rhyme
of circles survives like the story of a single tree unseen
unless chopped. The wind will soften its bark with moss,

the wind of many languages. The parrots too
can talk, Senegal grays and cockatoos. They say hello,
repeating themselves as parrots do,

and in the silences between when the parrots
do not speak, the trees do. You could say they sing
a circling song, or that they hum and do not sing at all.

[Éspanôl]

Below lasered skies of love, neoned by opportunities
and software, honkey porno flicks where vibrations
are slow and colorful, the lovers stare at their feet,
cornered by untranslatable intersections of pride or

grief that prevent them from seeing each other or
going anywhere but on this shoddy, advertised-blazed
curb whisked by taxi'd yellows where the soul preacher
microphones nervous salvations, and runaways roam

between mugshots of magazines, leathering and chaining
legs into monotonies of spent semen, and newspapers.
There is a tiny tulip-planted park in Hell's Kitchen and
benches beside the toweled bodybuilders who tan there

we could visit, surrounded by barrio delicatessens and
homesteaders bumped by rents. We could listen to tulips.

[Coronado]

There are no ancestors in California where I was born
on a naval base, only amphibious frogmen and sailors
who never stay in one place. I see them rim like lace
gray carriers or dive under mined blues to detonate or

jet swiftly from compressed airstrips, slowed by rips
of parachutes catching planes before they splash into
more blues. They all wore swabbie caps and stood up
straight when huge hulls creeked out or in, engined

anatomies crowded by organization and commands,
women waiting for them to come back to land. Today,
luck has changed, no woman's kept from the long seas,

ports of call and submarines that prowl mercurial
boundaries, too many of them, and fewer wait for ships
to come back from seas, widowwalked by reveries.

[Gutted]

Baccardi rum once gave my lupine canyons free run,
released luna moths to weave latticed tumbleweeds,
gave gophers speed over the sandy scorpions, a lonely
conservation under a sad and wasted sun that dropped

like a yolk into a water glass when the morning finally
came, queasy and green from those taranatula-haunted
sprees that make city life so fun and own-best-friendly,

then, seanced with resurrected benders, I was weened
from those desolate nipples that carried me through
despairing thirsts to breathe pale air and friends were
everywhere, bandaging my nerves, never doubting where

I came from, the shadowed caverns of the wolf, gophers
racing the pockmarked scorched salt earth that contains
and rewashes in refrains some out-of-sorts birth pain.

[Dark Age]

If only clouds, made from all colors but white,
were more surreal, tinctured, their bounced light
could haiku blight from garbaged vacant lots and
garden the underworld, the troubled skepticism

of children accepting tiny packets from thinning
men and dashing to and fro. We must be sued to
send plundered reliquaries back to Cyprus from
Indianapolis no less, its petrochemical grasp,

our globe-trotting antiquity dealers traveling
far and fast, as if we can't envision a Coca Cola
super nation dripping with enough cash to make

us hack down statues, steal stained glass, just to
buy milk or meat. Flames of Rome dance to these
violins, shifting ashes into the eyes of children.

[Pin Dots]

Names with less syllables than mine will lift
cracked stairwells from tenements and broom
them off, add a balcony or two for flimsied
clothespins only the welfare'd use, and replace

them, while the national endowment's moneymen,
without saying anything aloud, baseball-bat more
gays, censor-snipping naughty bedrooms, bad art.
Nothing is ever exact. Animals are not precise,

caved in clans on the Sheetrocked millenniums,
huddled above small hungry flames in furs of
the sacrificed. We firefly through a multitude

of these hollows, bringing tiny illuminations
that never stay in one cave long enough to die,
but pass in a bleariness that alerts the eye.

[Nova Spies]

I do not think extraterrestrial telescopes have
an eye on us but on the arching antelopes lovely
to see as they run from us, quickened curiosities
that need viewing now. And the intelligences that

craft such unimaginably piercing glass, which
separates every jungled green, also weep, do not
destroy. Their UFO's, still too supple to video,
slink well beyond Mars to peep tearlessly as we

proliferate our industries and drive the starved
toward ivory. On small islands, whaled for food,
economies swell. In large nylon deep-sea nets,

acres of fish flip and thrash. More than any supper
needs is heedless efficiency created by skill, but we
have yet to see telescopes, our nimble animals.

[Shop Talk]

Larkin favored jazz above the Beatles, a churchgoer,
a modest observer, we tread in reverence behind his
tattered posters and cycle-clips, his weedy pavements,
yet can we eclipse the fiery horror glimpsed at the

cauldron's edge, burn its final splutterings as of only
Mr. Kurtz sears the abyss with sight, less frightening
when trousered, that view, less vulnerable. Some reliable

stolidity will guide us through those pulsant blacks,
bring us back, eyes wide with clairvoyancy, from dark
journeys best battened down by fiction, apparently. Poo,

I'm out of this literary venue like a bat, convolutions
drive me mad and "mad I cannot be" says Barthes and he's
right, the pleasure of the text says good night, sheets
are crispy on the bed I made and remake again and again.

[Spare Time]

Like to lounge with Bill, his hands are floral and cruddy,
they sweep about like clumsy acrobats to illustrate
a particular memory of him behind his glasses looking
painfully attacked by intellectuals even though there

weren't any around. He'd jump and dart all questions
as if tanks rolled over tables toward his glasses, borrowed
monocles, to smash his nose. When a General Patton question
broke through, he'd gasp, as if he were placed in the wrong

chair and didn't know where to go. After the fun was done
he'd run, lantering his exits with worried urgency to find
an honest man, well not a man exactly, some shadow to

lead him to the subway where he could go far downtown,
very away. He beacons me, his heart a tiny fluttering in
my hands, I set it free, it bobs and flutters all round me.

[Migrant]

Oh so roomlessly the pillow cases lift off, featherings
heading south out of what was once a house, over jumbled
interstates of little towns, their lawns and creaks, their
awkward signs always made of hues that grate against

impressionistic ponds. They carry my bed away. They
carry my nightgown, my powders, creams and candles
over the biked pool halls and hardware stores, the mud-
backed frogs and bees, cats and dogs. Where do they go,

so white and cotton-like, why don't they bring me along?
But they don't. That other world I never see's not me,
loves lifted into it scars made by a very thin blade

across my heart, I stay apart in the grungy confusions
of bus fumes where the grit is dark and limousined, in
vestibules like mindshafts under Afrikaner greed.

[Transfers]

I was funny when young, my armchaired puppetdoms
filled playgrounds always being shifted around by
geographies. Girls seemed weird with their frilly
domesticities, not fast at tag like boys but good

at skip rope and jacks, we got to play very fast to
speed up outcomes. The yoyo pride and pogo sticks
that rarified gravity into only hops gobbled evenings
on the street, whoever wanted to come in and go

to sleep? we never did. I had a friend named Daphne
Ripple, very Joan Baez, she lived in the colonel's
house and wrote letters. It was a big day to take

the white socks off, only wear pumps, very adult,
very Nancy Drew. Now I have no white socks, no Easter
bonnet, eggs robin blue, no congregation confirmed to.

[Marooned]

Yow, another summons. What have I done now?
I mispronounced an ocean. But how was I to know
how it sounds until it was spoken? No matter,
I'm fined, I should've heard its sound in shells,

should have known as any swimmer knows who
swims the channel, greased black to keep body
heat intact, and not gone round colonizing oceans
with tacky vowels, mispronouncing the absence

of continents with such liberty, flattening waves
with gauche presumption, as if I don't understand
oceans, never took a dip or quavered through their

tumultuous thwacking swells, salt whips, mutinies,
communities of exiles. So I'm snubbed by peg-legged
seafarers, never to vanish on closures of foam.

[Mauka]

Swept up in theory, untouched in true (some day
I must make love a concession to you, outfielder,
though second base in the middle of nowhere, so
less exciting, will do, a second place, a diamond

oasis where shortstops can tag all the steals
until rookie'd above our shoulders), these codas
blanket me in gruff warmth when the turquoise
Makapuu'd waters winter and I'm out in the cold

although nothing is ever as cold as it once was,
splintered glass downed in gulps. Shutters slam
old me's out of chalets onto the bambi'd ski slope

where Hawaiians surf in slow easy turns and
fall first, to mosey in quiet Mauna Loas downhill,
as zippy little jocks a tenth my age boogie by.

[Downcast]

Depression, a burgeoning malady that acnes language
with neologisms, Tofranil, Prozac, Elavil, descends
in vague dankness into shade-drawn rooms, thoughts
so dangerous they destroy you when isolated and

depression isolates, encloses the tightwound mind
to ever tock, to cramp the ordinary with a thudding
clock, punishing you with more and more push-ups
for something you've never done, never intended to,

yet it becomes, in its bathrobed paralysis, factual,
cruel, vengeful. Any door lets you out, any knob or
key, yet it follows you, an umbrella with storms

beneath rather than above. It doesn't want company,
help, love, it has itself, spinning as a wheel offground
fears that do not exist, could never exist if found.

[Retreat]

Above browned-leaved, daddy-longlegged paths and
cracked stone stairs overgrown by weeds, passing
through a statue of white concrete is Jesus. I'm glad
his hair's still long. Alexander the Great commanded

his soldiers to shave, cleansing marches of vermin.
Not much has changed except subtle adjustments in
tweeds fashion urges, but religion doesn't read glossy
magazines, drink and smoke, flirt in the retouched

sundowns of sailboats, a nimbus of swimsuits and
adoration arranged by stylists. It escapes, always
escapes fashion in poverties of grace and repose.

Seasons break this Judaic heart, hurled through
a horrid divorce, flog it, torture its continued promise,
yet the mute statue forgives, brings constant peace.

[Flight Plans]

Our ardent aliases, yours alas, mine however, bash
crash against this reversible mirror like gnats, fall
into a water cup in colonies of the drowned to pattern
its surface until the tip of a spoon scoops us into

the trash, our accidents then swallowed by thirst,
alas however to reunite, evolutionized in the compost,
and spring like uncocooned dragonflies into more rooms,
why go on? the spray of some insecticide's bound to

zap us soon and meanwhile there are screens to avoid
in these buzzing miasmas threaded by Ariadne, to carry
us out into the huckleberries: "If you were an apple

tree and I was a cherry, would you marry me anyway,
would you have my berry?" what's the use? seems you'd
rather terrify me, wing me through bulb-lit zooms.

[Womb Water]

Quit. Print. Quit. Print. What to choose? Quit.
Dulled thunders of sun gold my limbs and lungs,
enumerated by Midas, lost to rainbows that never
color footsteps, only lonely vistas where all the

people stop and stare because Santa is coming,
Santas of air, reindeer, sleighs are just chimneys
away if you jinglebell your silly tears. Time to go
skinny-dipping where rhythm needs no underwear,

part the water spiders on the water there, move
through the formless green of ponds with fingers
closed to pull the body into motion with slow

revolutions of the arms while, underneath, tads
and trout nibble the toes in an arena of mountained
oaks without second homes or fishing poles.

[Yawn]

Don't tell me you never sleep with anybody, encaved
by the moon, a loner dude who only sees nudity through
its hush of light in pale-hued chiaroscuro, that I'm to
unclothe in this luminous zero like a cameo, broached

to your friends, for the sake of something universal,
without end, beautiful. Hmm, another sideshow I'm
boothed in with all my tattoos, freaked by scrutiny,
voodooed as an oddity with inked bouquets on my

thighs and "I love you's" needled onto my breasts,
pit vipers in the corridors around my eyes, vexing
hexagons above my wrists, sword-slashed valentines

on my forearms, all for the pale enveloping slight
shifts of shade in the moonlight lending soft contours
to what hides my bones, eternal as flesh denied.

[Taboo]

In timberland I take my stand as another biological
month rolls in, wetting my moods, unmentionables
in the Venetian hues of history. And, as the fire-
based blows of the monsoon fade, forbid the sale

of paper, particularly this paper, torn from shade
to make more paper, more than half of it crumpled,
tossed away. And you, moody mentor, revolve through
time in a similar manner yet have been denied

understanding, sorry to say. Thickets of diminished
rain forests burned for fast consumption separate
us, cannot be heaved into a moo of sameness, fields

of undisrupted greens. Those pastures gouge the wild
densities that keep us sane, as if a window between
redwood sees what can't be chopped, must be saved.

[Roe Wade]

No one wants an abortion and from an abortion
no one is saved, yet in all the precautions and
reprimands it seems women are still enslaved,
first by divisions that make argument a deadly

game, then by Washington that takes argument
away, leaving us still footing the pain, chained
to a moment we never arranged, couldn't, alone.

Yet we make ourselves feel as if we must beg
to reverse an unholy mistake that only we have
made because we are so reckless and vain, so

irresponsible, they should put us away rather
than profit from clinics ruining white adoptions
so the smallest soul may be saved. From us.
What happened to protection, the first loss?

[Soundless]

Low chariot of my soul, my little home, no flattened
face will ever find the wilted flowers so nameless
they make my body black inside, no blues will gray
that inconsolable hideaway, no love will ever hush

that cry in this dry afterlife. There's no more to say
aloud, I tumble like a limbless cloud to dissolve to
you, I am the sword and shroud, I break in two and
die, we are inseparable, mute, unrevised. You rushed

my coppered obstacles and scrambled through to a
slow no go, we did away with you, my intangible, my
population. I cry onto the nose of my cat. She misses

you, makes me do the things I'd do for you, wishes
you'd come back, out of your sack, all crimped and
devolved, flimsy clouds ribbed by my lonely love.

[Drenched]

Ho hum, no one to castrate today, I'm in a humdrum
no show rain-whacked summer lake phase, buckshot
drops splattering miniscule waves near slags of rocks
while all the mosquitoes are far away, folded in

their leaved cathedrals, humming hymns to deities
we underacknowledge. I'll swim with the girls in the
Pollocked pond till lightning shoos us safely from
sacred mishaps. We look like painted nudes Manet

would do, but why bother to describe this to you,
Houdini of the submerged trunk hour, bejeweled by
locks and chains, yanking magic into place like

a marvel while I wait breathlessly above to throw
my arms around your muscles and say "ooo, you're
wonderful," which I will do, thundered and nude.

[Undone]

I feel sidelined by raw courage, the way you jangle
your phone, your nonexistent ideas that fizzle into
adagios and eliminate the world, your husky accent
et cet, yet, your knack for misinterpretation leaves

me, like an ice sculpture, cold, bereft, melting into
a banquet from a silver tray until every groove is so
smooth I'm a translucent lump, dumped, dibbled down
until the next pickax chisels my face to wince above

the champagne and linen napkins, boiled shrimp and
capered cows, to make the hors d'oeuvres splendid.
Carry me away before I melt, we can refrigerate

together among the perishables, we can make do
in this dark chill, you can butter-knife my colorless
cheeks, restyle my hair, change my expression.

[Mimicries]

Eventful dust accumulates beside these diminishing
flames, as if the candle were a glowing cup, all its wax
burned away amid the oval speckled graves of gnats. Slow
lobs of saffrons wave this wooded stratosphere, they too

disappear into a spindrift haze, soft tyrannies of black
profile the faint moonlight. And should one muffled speck
of dust lift without a stamp into that starry envelope
and seal this love I have for you and carry it through

those milky vestibules, you will not be, as the gnats
surrounding me, lost, but will move as tremolos along
the waves of oceans to bathe the moonward swimmers,

save the storm–flown boats, and so, I brush away those
thimbly saviors whose busy flurries kept me company
in these low fires, lift them into less hurried lives.

[Lulled]

Thruway towns, frazzling compressions of whatnots,
their pancake palaces, body parts, laundromatic signs,
draw me away in depletions of supplies from driftwood
haunts of the seashell's call, undinal and unsurprised

by invention. The surf-shocked rocks that underlie proud
claims of every settlement still meet the bash of waves
unmoved. The tremulous salt sway that immures the earth
is contained by monodies of stone, so amid the clatterings

of parking stalls runs the thruway only surf prevents from
going on and on. I leave and return, heavy with commodities,
shower the visible from my body in U-turns of soap. The

stone night descends, stills mechanical errors of thought,
stubbly quandaries. It rocks the continent in me against
those bounding swells, fanned by loops of hungry gulls.

[Insurrections]

My blacks, once thick with density, thin to precisions
of deep gray. I miss their resistance, their irreverent
vulgarity. Like unkempt Goths, smashing barbarians
from these turreted views, they were crude and loyal.

They slunk back to feast in my halls, smelling of savagery,
the palace now a trumpet call to courtly civility, rondelles
of the masquerade, yet the barbarous must be quelled, so
civilizations say, to save these orderly realms from the

stench of clashing swords, their repression the mainstay
of the lordly, filigreed in fleur-de-lis. But beyond fallow
meadows, cragged and barren on the parched outreach

of hills where serfdoms are less assured, gruff grumblings
herd rebellions, shadow the matchsticked hamlets taxed
for distant ornaments, encircle grottos of hacked fire.

[Clasped]

Adriadne, we must stop this marvellous madness or
cliffs will rise to meet our innocence with jagged
indifference, stop this sleepy-eyed wailing for what
time never permits, unnatural stasis misinterpreted

as bliss. We must shake ourselves awake, stare clearly
into absence, that blank departed sea, and step back,
fall onto this earth that caressed our feet, we must
not fly for that wedded impossibility only to swing

a chapter shut on his glorious story, elude our bacchic
victory of the Pleiades to disappoint Taurus. That
would be too ungoddess of us, too daughterly, young,

we are ancient as the stone sandals we walk upon,
we bow to no shattering disloyalty, no other. Adriadne,
you cannot escape my hands for that carelessness.

[Cadenza]

Ah, if only my turn were up, you could take over,
Mensa man, screech your penknife on this glassy
slang and skitter a few more firemen up those
leggy ladders to bring down the suffocating but

I'm selfish, intense over my Scrabble squares,
polysyllabic, here in the weedy backyard, and
you (I believe I've said this roughly ninety times)
are missing, too bored to wait for me to make

my move, triple-square the delights out of you,
catch up, keep the game stimulating so I'll stop
accusing you of patronizing my overeducation.

Foo, I'm flipping this competition onto the grass
to crash in the plastic swimming pool and doze.
Oh, you've crowded my plan, how physical of you.

[Tidy]

I love laundry even though I don't do it myself,
the fresh smell of "separate and completely folded"
clothes when they come back from the laundromat
to be fluffed and neatly stacked in drawers. It's

worth the few extra bucks needed to delegate
this responsibility just to appreciate the labor
performed by anyone else; I work hard for money
to give it away. And all my hangers must be the

same length apart, makes my heart feel proudly
organized, too virgo for many but some like to
see same spaces between clothes. Who knows?

It's a privacy, a solitary celebration when wash
comes back from the laundry. I don't expect to be
understood, but like what's hidden to look good.

[Sidekicked]

I'm ballad bonkers, need to chill, watch a rerun,
pop a pill (ah, those diet days, trilling agitations),
calm down, rustle up an invitation, but I don't want
to leave you stranded in intercourse, kimosabe,

after the mountains you've moved to elude me,
let my true grit slip, unbraid, weasel out of this
impossible eternity we've made just because I'm
a little tuckered by time, what with the ho-dad

gunslingers yet to undermine among the mesas,
gentle genitalia unsaved from crime. That wouldn't
be sock-hop faithful. Say, I cowered away one awe–

expiring day because I was in trouble, you blasted
down the road in a major huff, I wasn't savable 'nuf
fer you then, hadn't found the beyond the bend.

[Stranded]

The neighbors die, flowers sprout from hospital beds,
a shady population spreads below the sunny floor. A door
bounces back, shouting their names in address books,
not erased in fact, but left to decode the evaporating

past, to bring their penmanship breath. In what hall of
moments did they spin, bump ordinary problems, sneak
late night snacks? what were their favorite foods, their
special colors, tie clips, scarves? what were the rings

they always wore for reasons only they knew, what
did they say that so soothed my mind at the time, what
was the time, where was the avenue? Why must I

jaywalk away, leave them behind on the rush-hour curb
gazing at the next block, waiting impatiently for the
sign to turn that never turns, never again says walk.

[Sanctum]

I don't know what I'm missing but please don't tell me,
I need a burglary not a message, bust in, rob my precious
spoons, rip out the electrical wiring, masked voyeur,
but don't drop postcards into the blue box instead of

coming over. I'm Victorian enough, hauntingly elusive,
laced, spaced on chamber music, doilies under every vase,
silk-embroidered pastel bouquets stitched and stitched,
but perhaps I'm not willowy enough to snatch from the

paternal autocrat, not flushed gracefully enough to escape
into your hands, perhaps, perhaps. Perhaps more postcards,
little keys and stamped immodesties are needed to free

me from this laden desk, but let's communicate less. Meet
me in Mystic where trains converge in this megalopolis, we'll
search the platform, our embrace will empty the tracks.

[Ghosts]

Translucent nuns sweep this kitchen. I trip over their
thin brooms. Teenage lost boys vampire the jelly jars
looking for pale chums, astral gals to telepath clutter,
make the plates swim and spin, fly through filaments

of rips ruffling the wind-whipped wide window in black
Transylvanian nights of the garlic necklace and silver
spike, coffins agape with missing missives, rice grains
changed to creepy maggots, the hail furious and wild.

Mischievous winds prick its voluminous haste. Forks
and spoons tornado the Teflon room. Wallpapered daisies
are shocked by the gloom, fingered awake by invisibles

that zoom through the cloistered cupboards. The nuns,
committed to the serene, sweep and sweep. The rooftop
screams in thunderbursts till dawn, hushed by daybreak.

[Makai]

So, the fogged crystal ball encloses my mosaics, mimosas
of the sun, mists the workshift schedules posted on the
trellis beside the mai tai'd men who've jumbo'd to my isle,
necklaced in gold charms white collars conceal; why be

a waitress anywhere else? why dress in black and white
in some dark bar when one can fetch requests in a bikini
by a reef, career plans put on indefinite hold? I fold the
paper napkins under the thumb-sized umbrella shading

the pineapple slice, vermilion cherry, and strut by them
deckchairs slow. I got a ways to go in this trade, on this
luxury-lapped patio, but I like the waves, a turquoise no

metal pins down, surf sets that catch warm weathers
in flushed sunsets, all jostled by group tours now, the wide
bright Duke Kahanumoku beach once called "miracle mile."

[Roundrobin]

Years lapsed, I skid the zodiac, banished grass, jiggled
kingdoms for chessmen, untangled my matted hair,
became intangible, hot with intruding seas, enclosed.
I disrobed, weary of galoshes and weather, learned what

a photographer knows, broke cameras with impatience,
overuse. And, now, in this aftermath of understanding
impossible to experience anywhere else, the visible
escapes, yet I'm not blind, just rusty. I can't picture

you sleeping. More globes must be encircled for that
transparency, a slow exposure without flash, and yet
I only travel in dreams, the flying carpet of geography

a coverlet for my bed, patterns of cultures, salutations.
It is late. The crickets separate. The candles burn, are
replaced. The night's become disoriented, middle-aged.

[Posted]

Transferring your list to the wall, an objet trouvé
of your persistence, all the names you love become
encased in space: dada data, rubric, retracing the
trinket-bare room with a hand moving as music

heard in the woods between trees, but, as always,
there is something wrong with the image locked
in this frameless encasement, a missing letter
misspelling the effect, humanizing it, flubbing it

up, so passing aesthetes, arguing that there is not
the correct intention to make your list a work of art,
would have to pause, reconsider the penmanship,

strange slurs of phonetics, forgotten consonants
in the crushed compression of southpaw script,
and muse for a moment, confused, and hesitant.

[Ethereal]

Vile Spring downbeats dread, your bubbly promises
drop dead, garlanding frail Ophelias in pale streams
offstage, but I like you anyway, your thorny rains,
your incoming tide of light unsettling the sleepy

schedules of unseen leaves, unraveling leggings,
keeping bees awake at night bumbling above tardy
impatiens. I must dress down for you, let the air
through snug seams, flip the minute hand full circle

in your favor, shoo those wintery weltanschauungs
out the bolted door, give them the boot. I am accused
of everything. Shoot, it's a drag, a constant tumble,

the guys are all mad, uptight, aroused by thrashing
traumas I have trouble being goo-goo eyed about.
I should just Ophelia away with the girl scouts, huh.

[Sweet Dreams]

Cryptic wisteria, that's an idea, I'll vine myself up
someone's legs. He will experience a vague flutter
like a lost continent below the sea. Crimson reefs
of molten lava surface as an unclaimed Eden through

his mind, nude and primeval, one rib too many, thrown
from a dream like a skipped stone rippling his thighs,
ripples rising and rising. I do not think birds will sing,
however. My imagery is too profusive. I'd boggle his

primeval thinking like a wrench. The machinery would
break down. I'd have to unvine fast before the entire
continent resinks, leaving but a puddle in its wake,

so don't tell me you're all ears, I know that game.
"Well, enough about my problems. What do you think
about my problems?" Excuse me, I'm falling asleep.

"Came there for cure, and this by that I prove,
Love's fire heats water, water cools not love."